D1529128

Sweaters for Dogs
Knitting Cozy and Lovely Sweaters for Your Puppies

Copyright © 2021

All rights reserved.

DEDICATION

Contents

Pink Sweater

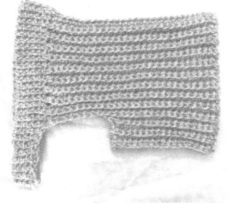

A few years, you might remember, I did a post on a crocheted dog sweater for our dog Snowflake. I'm still amazed at how many visits a day that post gets, and how many questions too! I could never answer most of the questions, however, since I was mainly flying by the seat of my pants as a new crocheter when I made that pattern!

So after a few years of making similar sweaters for Snowflake, I came up with this easier version and tutorial for basically the same pattern. Just modified - and better!

The great thing about this pattern is that it can be made to fit any size dog. Just take measurements as I wrote below, or try to guess some out using the dog size charts I've included. I worked pretty hard to put this all together, so I hope it's easy to understand and, most importantly, comes out great! If there are still questions, however, feel free to leave them in the comments!

So, here we go...

Measuring Your Dog

First, you'll need to make all of your measurements.You can either measure your own dog or use the handy charts above from Pet It Dog Apparel to guesstimate the measurements. If you have a larger dog, then you can probably find some estimated measurements with a quick search :) Here is what you need to measure, along with a chart I drew up that might help:

- Collar (around the neck, loosely)
- Back (from the collar to where you'd like the sweater to end)
- Back Girth (around the back, leave out the tummy)
- (D) Tummy girth (from side to side of the tummy, leg to leg)
- (E) Tummy length (from bottom of sweater length to front legs)

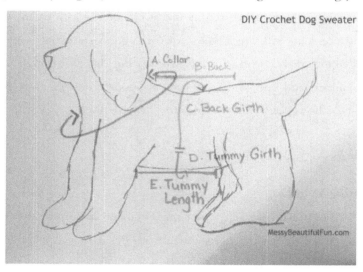

Now that you have your measurements, you can begin crocheting!

1. Cast on your yarn and make a chain the length of the Back (B) measurement. Be sure your back ends at a good point for both the tummy and back - as in, you don't want your dog weeing on the sweater, so don't make it too long ;)

2. Now you can use any stitch pattern you'd like to create the back of the sweater. I single crocheted in back loops only to make mine. I like making this sort of pattern because it makes the sweater stretchier. Crochet in each chain across.

3. Now continue to crochet in each stitch across until you have a rectangle piece measuring the length of your (C)Back Girth measurement (as in the photo above). This is the top of your sweater that will cover your dog's back.

4. Now you're going to create the tummy portion. Begin to crochet in the next row as you have been, but don't go to the end - only go until you reach you (E) Tummy Length measurement. Stop here and turn your work.

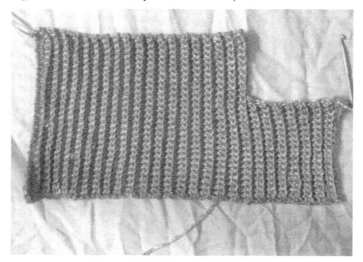

5. Chain 1, and continue your stitch pattern on these shorter rows until you make

this small square your (D)Tummy Girth measurement. You can what I mean in the picture above. Now you have to body of your sweater.

6. Now you'll sew the two ends together using your hook. Fold the tummy square over to the other side of the sweater so it looks like the picture above. Using your hook slip stitch the sides together. You can also choose to cast off first and sew the two sides together with a yarn hook, but I prefer this way since it's simpler and makes cleaner lines.

7. Now you'll be making your collar. Go to the front of your seater where the big opening is. Attach your yarn to the top of the rows (as shown) and crochet into the top of each row across. When you reach the end, chain enough stitch so that this whole side will measure the length of your (A) Collar measurement. Be sure to leave some extra lag here since you don't want it to be too tight if your dog ever gets stuck on something.

8. Once you have your length, attach your chain to the other side of the collar, where you attached your yarn. You now have a big circle the length of the collar measurement. Now you'll continue to crochet in rounds until the collar is as high as you'd like it to be. You can do one layer as I did, or you can make it longer and folded   over.

And that's all there is to make this little sweater for your dog. As you can see, it's super easy to make for any size dog and can easily be adjusted with different stitch patterns to make it however you'd like. Of course, you could also add some cute buttons,   embroidery,   or   mix   up   different   colors   of   yarn.

I'm including a few graphics down here to help you out in remembering the steps so you can Pin them for later. Once you've made this sweater once it's actually really easy to make again and again!

Chihuahua Sweater

Last night I sat up in bed working on a crochet sweater to fit this little guy. He enjoys it so much that he fell asleep while I took his picture.

My Chihuahua's Measurements

Chest = 15 1/2 inches.

Neck = 10 1/2 inches.

Waist 12 1/2 inches.

Shoulder blades to base of tail = 14 inches.

You can try this project on your chihuahua as you work.

Materials Required:

4.5mm Crochet hook.

Row markers.

Darning needle.

Red Heart Super Saver Stripes Yarn. Medium 4. Colour Cool Stripe.

2X 1 inch buttons.

1 Larger button (optional for collar).

Gauge:

Using a measuring tape

Approximately 4 rows = 2 inches.

Approximately 6 hdc = 2 inches.

I measured my gauge on body of finished project.

I've included some measurements along the way.

Special Abbreviations:

Ch = Chain.

Sc = Single Crochet.

Ea = Each.

St(s) = Stitch(es).

Mnr = Mark New Row/Round.

Rnd(s) = Round(s).

Beg = Beginning.

Ss = Slip Stitch.

Hdc = Half Double Crochet.

Bl = Back Loop.

Instructions:

Starting with the collar.

Row 1: Ch 20. Turn. Hdc in 2nd ch from hook. Hdc in ea ch across. (19hdc)

Rows 2-18: Ch 2. Turn. Hdc in ea bl across, forming 'hills and valleys'. (19hdc)

Collar should measure approximately 5 1/2 inches X 10 inches.

Fold project in half, lining row 1 evenly up to row 18. Evenly ss through bl of both rows at same time, forming a tube (collar).

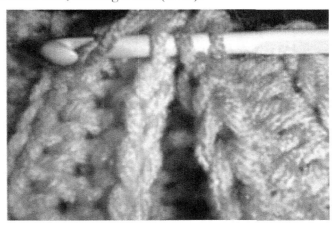

Working right to left, ss 6 times across to next 'hill'.

The Body:

Row 1: Ch 2. *Hdc in next st. Hdc in next valley, hdc in next st, hdc in next hill.* Repeat from * to * 6 more times. Hdc in next hill. (28hdc)

Row 2: Ch 2. Turn. Hdc in next 12 sts. Ch 4. Sk next 4 sts (Forming leash hole). Hdc in next 12 sts. (24hdc)

Rows 3-6: Ch 2. Turn. Hdc in ea st across. (28hdc)

Project should measure approximately 10 inches across.

Row 7: Ch 2. Turn. Hdc in ea st across. Ch 21. (28hdc, 21ch)

Row 8: Turn. Hdc in 2nd ch from hook. Hdc in ea ch and st across. (47hdc)

Row 9: Ch 2. Turn. Hdc in next 44 sts. Ch 1. Sk next st (Forming button hole). Hdc in last 2 sts. (46hdc)

Row 10: Ch 2. Turn. Hdc in ea st across. Sk last st. (46hdc)

Row 11: Ch 2. Turn. Hdc in next 43 sts. Ch 1. Sk next st (Forming a button hole). Hdc in last 2 sts. (45hdc)

Row 12: Ch 2. Turn. Hdc in ea st across. Sk last st. (45hdc)

Strap should measure approximately 16 inch long with 2 button holes.

Row 13: Ch 2. Turn.Hdc in next 22 sts. (22hdc)

Rows 14-18: Ch 2. Turn. Hdc in ea st across. (22hdc)

Row 19: Turn. Hdc in ea st across. Sk last st. (21hdc)

Row 20: Repeat Row 19. (19hdc)

Row 21: Repeat Row 19. (17hdc)

Row 22: Repeat Row 19. (15hdc)

Row 23: Repeat Row 19. (13hdc)

Row 24: Repeat Row 19. (11hdc)

Round 1: Ch 1 (mnr). Turn. Evenly sc around. Ss in beg ch 1 to join. (168sc)

Fasten off. Weave in ends.

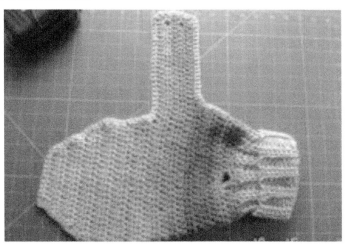

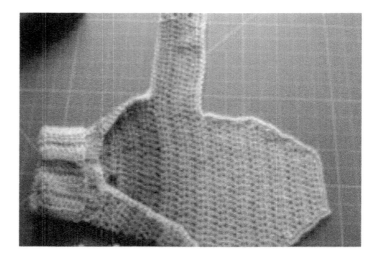

Try the sweater on your model. Line up the strap and sew buttons in place. I also added a button to the collar just for looks.

Easy Small Dog Sweater

So, first off, here's a little background on how this pattern came to be.

About six years ago my parents decided to move out to the wilds of Idaho. And I do mean "wilds" folks. They traded in the hustle and bustle of the city to live a quiet simple country life.

They chose to settle down in a remote region of northeastern Idaho in 400 sq foot cabin with no running water and no electricity. They raise goats, chickens, and ducks on their 15-acres of country bliss.

Not to mention mom's fabulous garden in which she grows the biggest and best crops I have ever seen or tasted! I like to call it "the farm". But it is really more of a homestead and I love it out there.

I made my first visit about three years ago near the end of the summer. It was warm, beautiful, quiet, and much too brief. I returned the following year to stay for the summer and brought my two precious little Yorkshire Terriers with me.

Jack and Jake, my Yorkie babies, had as much fun as I did. Maybe more! They spent their days chasing squirrels, chickens, and deer. I spent lazy mornings walking the property with the boys, enjoying mom's cooking on the outside grill, and evenings listening to the wolves howl. True story.

But as the summer nears to a close, Idaho weather can get chilly, as Jack, Jake, and I discovered. I, fortunately, came armed with coats. My boys, however, did not.

Now there is a lot of controversy over "dressing up" animals and I must admit that before I got Yorkies I was dead set against it. For heaven's sake, clothes are for people!

You may think that now, but wait until you watch your little ones shake & shiver in the nippy breeze and you'll change your mind pretty quick.

Just FYI folks, Yorkies have hair, not fur. It does not keep them warm. As a responsible pet parent, I felt it was my duty to crochet them some warm winter sweaters.

[list style="style6"] [li]This pattern is available as a large print, ad-free, printable PDF pattern.

SUMMARY:

This quick and easy small dog crochet sweater is warm and stylish. Crocheted with a beautifully patterned wool blend yarn it will keep your little fur babies fashionable and cozy during the chilly autumn and winter months. Plus, it's super easy to put together! Even the newest of crochet beginners can do it, I promise.

DIFFICULTY LEVEL: LEVEL 1 – BEGINNER

FINISHED DIMENSIONS:

- Back measures about 9 1/2-inches from neck to end.
- Chest measures about 6-inches from neck to belly.

GAUGE:

13 stitches and 4 rows = 4 – inches in double crochet

MATERIALS:

- Crochet Hook size J-6mm
- **Lion Brand Amazing Strawberry Fields** (53-Percent Wool, 47-Percent Acrylic)

Note: yarn is 4 Medium Worsted-weight, Afghan, Aran Yarn; 1-3/4-Ounce (50 g), 147 yd (135 m)

ABBREVIATIONS:

Stitch (St)

Chain stitch (ch)

Slip-stitch (slp st)

Single crochet (sc)

Double crochet (DC)

Back post only (BPO)

Single crochet 2 together (Sc2tog) – This is called making a decrease and it is actually very easy to do! So, please don't be put off by this. You can do it! Click the link for the tutorial.

NOTE: Pictures for tutorial below shown in **Red Heart Super Saver – print Bon Bon**.

BACK:

~ Start at the neckline and work towards the tail.

Chain 31

Row 1: DC in 2nd ch from hook working in the BPO and then across (30 sts).

Rows 2: Ch 2, turn work, DC in 1st DC from hook and then across (30 sts)

Row 3: Repeat row 2.

~ Do not bind off. Fold collar in half lengthwise, SC through both halves across the bottom to seal the collar. when you reach the end, do not bind off, simply go ahead to row 4.

Row 4: Ch 2, turn work, DC across.

Rows 5 –18: Repeat row 4.

Row 19: Ch2, turn work, Sc2tog the first two stitches, Dc across, Sc2tog the last two stitches. (28 sts)

~ Each time you Sc2tog it reduces your stitch count by one. Since you did it twice in row 19, your stitch count should now be 28 sts.

Row 20: Repeat row 19. (26 sts)

Row 21: Ch 2, turn work, Dc in the next 12 stitches, Sc2tog the next two stitches, Dc in the last 12 stitches. (24 sts)

Bind off & weave in ends.

CHEST:

~ Start at belly end and crochet towards the neck.

Chain 18

Row 1: DC in the 2nd ch from hook and in each ch across. (17 sts)

Rows 2 – 5: Ch 2, turn work, DC across.

Rows 6 – 13:   Ch2, turn work, Sc2tog the first two stitches, Dc across, Sc2tog the last two stitches.

~ Remember this reduces your stitch count by two for each row because you have Sc2tog twice.

Row 14: There should be only 2 stitches left. Sc2tog these last 2 stitches.

Bind off & weave in ends.

~ The chest piece should essentially be a triangle shape.

ASSEMBLY:

- Place chest piece in the center of back pieces with right sides together. The tip of the chest piece should be at the base of the neck. So that when the chest piece is seamed in, there will a slight opening in the neck.
- Use slip-stitch (slp st) to seam together the slight opening in the neck.
- Use slip-stitch (slp st) to seam in the chest piece.

29

- Leave about a 2-inch hole on each side for legs.

~ I used my dogs as models to figure out where to make the holes, but in general, they were about 5-6 inches from the neckline.

NOTE: Sweaters are machine washable, but do not exceed 400C water temperature.

I think my boys just look so dashing in their warm and cozy sweaters!

We go back to Idaho every year, sometimes more than once a year. Usually in the spring and summer when the grass is green and the flowers are in bloom, but every once in a while we make a cool autumn or snowy winter trip.

And I never forget to bring the boys coats to keep them nice and toasty!

I hope you enjoy this easy pattern as much as I did and your little ones love their coats too!

Best wishes & happy crocheting!

Easy Dog Sweater Pattern

We have three dogs in our house; one 5lb, one 13lb, and one half Pitbull/half Dachshund that absolutely runs the show. I mean really, with those eyes and her tiny little legs?! She's simply majestic. ♥

This stylish crochet dog sweater pattern comes in sizes XS, S, and M, and is worked from the neck down, all in one piece with no sewing involved. If you need the crochet sweater for large dogs.

For this dog sweater we are using Brava Worsted yarn. My colors here are Dove Heather, Paprika, and Avocado. You could substitute with any worsted you have on hand, as it doesn't take much – especially for the extra small dog sweater.

Materials:

Brava Worsted Weight Yarn
-approx. 110 yards for XS
-approx. 205 yards for S
-approx. 375 yards for M

Crochet hook in size H/5mm

Size ~	Neck ~ (up to)	Chest (up to)
XS	8"	14"
S	12"	18"
M	15"	24"

Gauge: 14 sts x 13 rows = 4"

Gauge pattern:

Row 1: Ch-18. (sc, dc) in 2nd ch from hook. * sk next ch, (sc, dc) in next * repeat between * * 6 more times. Sk next ch, sc in last. (17)

Rows 2 – 14: Ch-1, turn, * (sc, dc) in next st, sk next st * repeat between * * 7 more times. Sk next st, sc in last. (17) Measure for gauge.

Note on gauge: Always make your swatch slightly larger than it needs to be so that when you measure you are only including inside stitches, not the outside stitches that are not uniform in shape. More on gauge here.

Pattern notes:

Pattern written using US terms.

The chain at the beginning of the row does not count as a stitch.

Front post/Back post stitches are used for the collar.

The body of this sweater uses the Thicket (aka Suzette) stitch.

Now that you've got gauge down, its time to whip up a dog sweater! If you need the crochet sweater for large dogs.

Collar:

Row 1: Fhdc– (33, 43, 53) (or ch- (34, 44, 54), hdc in 2nd chain from hook and in each to end.) Join to top of first st with sl st. Stitch count: (33, 43, 53)

Row 2: Ch-1, do not turn, * fphdc around next st, bphdc around next st * repeat between * * around, fphdc around last st. Join to top of first fphdc with sl st. Stitch count: (33, 43, 53)

Row 3: Ch-1, turn, * bphdc around next st, fphdc around next st * repeat between * * around, bphdc around last st. Join to top of first bphdc with sl st. Stitch count: (33, 43, 53)

Row 4: Ch-1, turn, * fphdc around next st, bphdc around next st * repeat between * * around, fphdc around last st. Join to top of first fphdc with sl st. Stitch count: (33, 43, 53)

Rows 5 through (6, 8, 10): alternate rows 3 & 4. Stitch count: (33, 43, 53)

Chest/Body:

Row (7, 9, 11): Ch-1, do not turn. (sc, dc) in first st. * sk next st, (sc, dc) in next * repeat between * * around, sk next, (sc, dc, sc) in last st. Join to top of first sc with sl st. Stitch count: (35, 45, 55)

Row (8, 10, 12): Ch-1, turn, (sc, dc) in first st. * sk next st, (sc, dc) in next * repeat between * * around, sk next, (sc, dc, sc) in last st. Join to top of first sc with sl st. Stitch count: (37, 47, 57)

Rows (9, 11, 13) through (13, 17, 25): repeat previous row. Stitch count: (47, 61, 83)

Row (14, 18, 26): Ch-1, turn, (sc, dc) in first st. * sk next st, (sc, dc) in next * repeat between * * around (do not do the extra sc). Join to top of first sc with sl st. Stitch count: (48, 62, 84)

Armholes:

Row (15, 19, 27): Ch-1, turn * sk next st, (sc, dc) in next * repeat between * * (0,1, 2) more times. (2, 4, 6 sts total so far). Sk next st, sc in next. Ch-(7, 11, 15), sk-(9, 13, 17) sts. In next sc, place (sc, dc). Repeat between * * (10, 11, 17) more times. Sk next st, sc in next. Ch-(7, 11, 15), sk-(9, 13, 17) sts. In next sc, place (sc, dc). Repeat between * * to end. Join to top of first sc with sl st. Stitch count: (44, 58, 80)

Row (16, 20, 28): Ch-1, turn. * Sk next st, (sc, dc) in next * repeat between * * around (including chains). Join to top of first sc with sl st. Stitch count: (44, 58, 80)

Rows (17, 21, 29) through (20, 30, 44): Ch-1, turn, * sk next st, (sc, dc) in next * repeat between * * around. Join to top of first sc with sl st. Stitch count: (44, 58, 80)

Begin body tapering:

Row (21, 31, 45): Ch-1, turn, sl st in first (2, 4, 6,) sts, * sk next st, (sc, dc) in next * repeat between * * (18, 23, 32) more times. Sk next st, sc in next. (leave remaining 2, 4, 6) sts unworked) Stitch count: (39, 49, 67) not including sl sts.

Row (22, 32, 46): Ch-1, turn, sk first 2 sts, * (sc, dc) in next, sk next st * repeat between * * (17, 22, 30) more times. Sc in next st. Stitch count: (37, 47, 63)

Row (23, 33, 47): Ch-1, turn, sk first 2 sts, * (sc, dc) in next, sk next st * repeat between * * (16, 21, 29) more times. Sc in next st. Stitch count: (35, 45, 61)

Continue decreasing until you reach row (36, 46, 66) ending with (9, 19, 23) sts.

Row (37, 47, 67): Ch-1, turn, sc in each st/row end around.

Cabled Dog Sweater

If you've arrived here via the Lion Brand Yarn Heros charity campaign, welcome! If not, click on the graphic below to meet all of the Yarn Heroes and learn about their awesome designs for charity!

"Well, that didn't work. She just put me up on this thing instead. Apparently the chair was too comfortable."

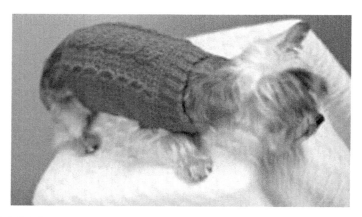

MATERIALS

- Yarn: Worsted Weight /4 / 100 – 200 yards *(yarn shown in the sample is Lion Brand Yarn Wool-Ease Yarn, Denim)*
- Crochet Hook: H/8/5.00mm, or size needed to obtain gauge (My favorite crochet hooks are the Clover Amour Hooks, I've never had an ache in my hand since switching)
- Scissors
- Yarn Needle
- Stitch Markers

Many of these materials are available for purchase through our affiliates below:

DIFFICULTY

- Intermediate

SIZES

- XS: Neck 8-9.5"; Girth 11-12.5"; Back Length 8"
- S: Neck 10-11.5"; Girth 13-15"; Back Length 10"
- M: Neck 12-13.5"; Girth 15.5-17"; Back Length 12"
- L: Neck 14-15.5"; Girth 19-21.5"; Back Length 14"

GAUGE

- Neck: 6 sts x 6.75 rows = 1.5"
- Body of Sweater: 6.5 sts x 6.5 rows = 2"

ABBREVIATIONS (US TERMS)

- ch(s): chain(s)
- yo: yarn over
- sl st: (slip stitch)
- sc: single crochet
- fpdc: front post double crochet
- bpdc: back post double crochet
- fptr: front post treble crochet
- ext sc: extended single crochet
- st(s): stitch(es)
- RS: Right Side
- FLO: front loop only
- BLO: back loop only
- FWD Cbl A (6 strand cable):

SPECIAL STITCHES

- **Extended Single Crochet (ext sc):** Insert hook into stitch indicated, yo, pull up a loop, yo, pull thru 1 loop on hook, yo, pull thru remaining 2 loops on hook.

- **Front Post Treble Crochet (fptr):** Yo 2 twice, insert hook from front to back to front around the post of the designated stitch, yo, pull up a loop, (yo, pull thru 2 loops) 3 times.

- **Forward Cable A (FWD Cbl A):** Skip next 3 post sts, fptr around next 3 post sts, working in front of fptr just worked, fptr around each skipped post st.

INSTRUCTIONS

Changes for Sizes Written as Follows: X-Small (Small, Medium, Large)

NECK

Row 1 (RS): Ch 7, sc in 2nd ch from hook and in each ch across. Turn. *(6 sts)*

Row 2: Ch 1, BLO sl st in each st across. Turn.

Row 3: Ch 1, BLO sc in each st across. Turn.

Rows 4 – 37 (43, 49, 55): Rep Rows 2 – 3.

Row 38 (44, 50, 56): With the RS facing out, bring the 1st row to meet the last row. Position your working yarn so that it's on the inside of the neck. Ch 1, (Insert your hook from front to back into the FLO of the 1st st of Row 1, insert your hook from back to front into the BLO of the 1st st of the last row, yo, pull thru all loops to complete sl st) repeat across. Do not fasten off. Continue on to Neck Edging.

NECK EDGING

Rnd 1 (RS): Ch 1, sc into the side of each row around the neck. Join w/ sl st to 1st st. *(38, 44, 50, 56 sts)*

Rnds 2 [(2 – 3) (2 – 3) (2 – 4)]: Ch 1, sc in each st around. Join.

Do not fasten off. Continue on to Body of Sweater.

BODY OF SWEATER

Row 1(RS): Ch 1, 2 ext sc in first st, ext sc in next 20 (26, 32, 38) sts, 2 ext sc in next st. Turn. *(24, 30, 36, 42 sts)*

Row 2: Ch 1, 2 ext sc in first st, ext sc in next 2 (5, 8, 11) sts, bpdc around next st, ext sc in next st, bpdc around next st, ext sc in next 3 sts, bpdc around next 6 sts, ext sc in next 3 sts, bpdc around next st, ext sc in next st, bpdc around next st, ext sc in next 2 (5, 8, 11) sts, 2 ext sc in last st. Turn. *(26, 32, 38, 44 sts)*

Row 3: Ch 1, 2 ext sc in first st, ext sc in next 3 (6, 9, 12) sts, skip next 2 sts, fptr around next post st, ext sc in skipped ext sc, fptr around skipped post st, ext sc in next 3 sts, FWD Cbl A, ext sc in next 3 sts, skip next 2 sts, fptr around next post st, ext sc in skipped ext sc, fptr around skipped post st, ext sc in next 3 (6, 9, 12) sts, 2 ext sc in last st. Turn. *(28, 34, 40, 46 sts)*

Row 4: Ch 1, 2 ext sc in first st, ext sc in next 4 (7, 10, 13) sts, bpdc around next post st, ext sc in next st, bpdc around next post st, ext sc in next 3 sts, bpdc around next 6 post sts, ext sc in next 3 sts, bpdc around next post st, ext sc in next st, bpdc around next post st, ext sc in next 4 (7, 10, 13) sts, 2 ext sc in last st. Turn. *(30, 36, 42, 48 sts)*

Row 5: Ch 1, ext sc in next 6 (9, 12, 15) sts, fpdc around next post st, ext sc in next st, fpdc around next post st, ext sc in next 3 sts, fpdc around next 6 post sts, ext sc in next 3 sts, fpdc around next post st, ext sc in next st, fpdc around next post st, ext sc in last 6 (9, 12, 15) sts. Turn.

Row 6: Ch 1, ext sc in next 6 (9, 12, 15) sts, bpdc around next post st, ext sc in next st, bpdc around next post st, ext sc in next 3 sts, bpdc around next 6 post sts, ext sc in next 3 sts, bpdc around next post st, ext sc in next st, bpdc around next post st, ext sc in last 6 (9, 12, 15) sts. Turn.

Adjustments for Girth: If you need to adjust the sweater girth, you can do so at the end of Round 7 where you chain X. Simply add or subtract chains as needed to adjust the girth.

Round 7: Ch 1, ext sc in next 6 (9, 12, 15) sts, skip next 2 sts, fptr around next post st, ext sc in skipped ext sc, fptr around skipped post st, ext sc in next 3 sts, FWD Cbl A, ext sc in next 3 sts, skip next 2 sts, fptr around next post st, ext sc in skipped ext sc, fptr around skipped post st, ext sc in last 6 (9, 12, 15) sts, loosely ch 11 (12, 13, 22). Join w/ a sl st to the 1st st of the round. Turn. *(41, 48, 55, 70 sts)*

Round 8: Ch 1, ext sc in each ch, ext sc in each st to next post st, bpdc around next post st, ext sc in next st, bpdc around next post st, ext sc in next 3 sts, bpdc around next 6 post sts, ext sc in next 3 sts, bpdc around next post st, ext sc in next st, bpdc around next post st, ext sc in each remaining st around. Join. Turn.

Round 9: Ch 1, ext sc in each st to next post st, fpdc around next post st, ext sc in next st, fpdc around next post st, ext sc in next 3 sts, fpdc around next 6 post sts, ext sc in next 3 sts, fpdc around next post st, ext sc in next st, fpdc around next post st, ext sc in each remaining st around. Join. Turn.

Round 10: Ch 1, ext sc in each st to next post st, bpdc around next post st, ext sc in next st, bpdc around next post st, ext sc in next 3 sts, bpdc around next 6 post sts, ext sc in next 3 sts, bpdc around next post st, ext sc in next st, bpdc around next post st, ext sc in each remaining st around. Join. Turn.

Round 11: Ch 1, ext sc in each st to next post st, skip next 2 sts, fptr around next post st, ext sc in skipped ext sc, fptr around skipped post st, ext sc in next 3 sts, FWD Cbl A, ext sc in next 3 sts, skip next 2 sts, fptr around next post st, ext sc in skipped ext sc, fptr around skipped post st, ext sc in each remaining st around. Join. Turn.

Round 12: Ch 1, ext sc in each st to next post st, bpdc around next post st, ext sc in next st, bpdc around next post st, ext sc in next 3 sts, bpdc around next 6 post sts, ext sc in next 3 sts, bpdc around next post st, ext sc in next st, bpdc around next post st, ext sc in each remaining st around. Join. Turn.

Rounds 13 – ??: Repeat Rounds 9 – 12 until sweater measures 8" (10", 12", 14") & ending w/ an even number round repeat.

Last Round: Ch 1, sc in each st around. Join.

Fasten off. Weave in ends.

Sweaters for Dogs

Made in the USA
Middletown, DE
25 June 2022

67781494R00036